TALES OF A TRAVELLING POTTER
John Bourdeaux

Enjoy Life

John

June 2018

Tales of a Travelling Potter

© John Bourdeaux 2018
Cover Design: Tean Bourdeaux

Printed & Published by:
The St Ives Printing & Publishing Company,
High Street, St Ives, Cornwall TR26 1RS, UK.

ISBN 978-0-948385-95-7

*'Travel leaves you speechless ...
and then turns you into a Storyteller!'*

Tales of a Travelling Potter

John Bourdeaux

Acknowledgement

Thanks to Tean Bourdeaux for the cover design and to Fiona for all her help in editing and typing.

To all the family and friends who have so helpfully facilitated our travels.

Especial thanks to Margaret for her fortitude and support over the past forty-eight exciting years (certainly a girl in a million).

Contents

The Author

JOHN BOURDEAUX is a seventy two year old potter and artist living and working in one of the most beautiful islands in the world. The islands are situated twenty eight miles off Land's End in the far southwest of England, they are a paradise of white sandy beaches, fantastic wildlife and friendly Islanders who live happy simple lives well protected from the stresses and strains of mainland life.

John has been privileged to have gained an international reputation for his work over the past forty years. With the love of his life Margaret – his bride of forty eight years – they have spent their moderate savings on travel, helped considerably by various contacts in the travel industry who have helped them to achieve their aims.

However their travels are rarely straightforward as you will discover from the following series of articles.

The Acunpuncture Experience
The Svengali-esque Borat

AS MANY OF YOU may know, I have been experiencing severe pain over the past year in both knees. In wanting not to resort to a surgical solution, I have tried many solutions with minimal success, pain killers, ice packs, deep heat and many other suggested remedies to the extent of hanging a bag of corks on the end of my bed! But alas all to no avail. God forbid, one child general practitioner even suggested losing weight …

However, today is the day, 24th December 2017 cruising in the Baltic on a modern large luxurious ship. They have a spa that helps you cure all known ills, back problems, general health skin treatment, Yoga etc. Glory behold they even have a specialist acupuncturist, could he or she cure my painful knees?

With great trepidation I rang the Spa … Yes, a very attractive voice answered "I am sure we can help, however, you will need a consultation". She carried on to say that "there would be a free of charge consultation". So at 2 pm on Christmas Eve I presented myself at the desk on the lido deck with great apprehension. And hope (as by now I am certain a cure is going to be forthcoming). My beloved Margaret, to whom I am married, came with me for this first appointment as over the years I seem to somehow get into difficult situations without her. She certainly is my rock and without her I certainly can't exist away from my studio in the Isles of Scilly.

Briefly to introduce myself, I am a seventy two year old potter and artist, moderately overweight, self-conscious and away from the studio a very private person. Thanks to the wonderful Isles of Scilly and my fantastic barn studio where we have now lived for forty years I have managed with the help and support of our customers and visitors to gain an international reputation. This enables us to travel the world for four months of the year and work hard potting and painting for the other eight months.

I should add that this lifestyle was made possible by the freehold purchase in 1978 of a completely derelict barn from Prince Charles, who in those days had a benevolent land Steward who tried to help all the young Islanders.

Anyway, I digress …

We were shown into a small darkened consulting room with a very gentle background soothing music, a subtle smell of Joss sticks pervaded the air, to be joined a few minutes later by a Svengali type person, with great similarity to Borat, moustached and bearded with a hypnotic voice. (Indeed, actually a very calming experience).

Having summarily prodded my knees, he was delighted to inform us that he could undoubtedly help. It would need six treatments which he could fit in before the end of the cruise (how convenient). "How much?" I enquired. "£93 per session" he replied with a totally calm voice. Slightly stunned I decided to have the three sessions with a ten percent discount and then to continue if I felt an improvement, (which I surely would at this price), so handing over my AMEX card the deed was done. So there and then the first treatment started - pins in knees, feet and hands. After an hour, we were ushered out and an appointment made for the next day. (Christmas at sea, never to be forgotten).

Christmas arrived and apart from the force ten gales all was well. At 2 pm, off I went to the Spa on my own as due to the previous day I am now in my comfort zone. Presenting myself at the desk, I was met by a new receptionist, I think from Botswana, charming but perhaps lacking in a little English comprehension, however, extremely confident despite her intransigence.

I am now ushered into an altogether different consulting room (more like a room in a Roman villa, with fairly explicit statues and a couple of Botticelli paintings, the music now much more sensual). Perhaps, this acupuncture did have something to help this aging xenophobic potter. I duly prepared myself for the treatment to come, off socks and shoes, removing my trousers to bare my knees for the treatment to begin, modestly covering my brand new floral boxer shorts with a large towel.

The door opens and what a surprise! A very, very smart Asian lady enters the room dressed in an immaculate white nurse's uniform. My goodness; this acupuncture is getting better by the minute!

However, I feel a little awkward in my present attire and indeed she looks a little disconcerted. After the introductions (somewhat stilted), she suggests that the consultation gets underway. Surprisingly no needles in sight.

"Now Gerald", she says "how long have you been having these problems?"

Not wishing to be confrontational I accepted the name Gerald for the time being (I would correct this later).

"Well, it's been coming on for the past couple of years".

Taking in my failing physique, she surprisingly asked am I happily in a relationship and what other steps had I tried to solve my understandingly distressing situation … (at last someone who understands how painful my knees have been).

Well I retort, "the deep heat helps a lot and sometimes a hot bath is beneficial" (she looks slightly bemused, still no needles).

"How about some soft porn?" Having been married to a practice nurse, I had never thought this would help my knees?

A knock on the door and my Botswanan receptionist has a fairly animated conversation with my therapist. They both look in my direction, was my attire that premature for the acupuncture? Perhaps so, with abject apologies and total embarrassment, the therapist explains that due to a small administrative mistake, with regular receptionists off duty, my delightful Botswanan had booked me into the erectile disfunction clinic …

Oh well, I will try again tomorrow … whatever that brings!

Caracas – 1975
Crocodile Tears

GETTING TO AND TRAVELLING from the Caribbean in the early 1970's was never easy. However, it was well worth the effort despite a thirteen hour journey on a DC10 aircraft to St Lucia via a stopover in Barbados where the passengers were treated well. The cabin crew were helpful and professional, even travelling in economy was a pleasure. Despite the fact that we were travelling with two children under five, the journey was a delight and indeed a great adventure.

After a week acclimatising in a brand new hotel in St Lucia called La Toc, we readied ourselves for the real adventure, sailing round the Caribbean albeit on a vessel recently launched, called the *Cunard Princess*.

St Lucia in those days was not particularly welcoming to visitors, as one would be kept waiting in bars and served last, or totally ignored in shops, generally treated with disdain wherever we went. Indeed, several other guests were openly abused in Castries, the capital city. I think we were somewhat sheltered by the attraction of our two small children. We have visited St Lucia several times in the past few decades and in certain parts not a lot has altered.

However, we set sail but sadly the boat was a nightmare, no children's facilities as advertised, and an obsequious cabin steward who stole several items from us. As in many of our later sea journeys, force ten tropical winds seemed to follow our path and I, the only true sailor of the family, was seasick!

Our ports of call were exciting, Barbados, Grenada, Puerto Rico, Venezuela, Antigua and St. Thomas in the Virgin Islands.

The one highlight of the cruise was dressing for dinner every night. Full evening dress, white dinner jacket, bow ties and cummerbunds were the norm. No admittance to the Dining Room or any other public space after six pm. How things have altered, on a recent trip only the waiters were dressed in this fashion.

We decided that life in an inside cramped cabin was not for us, so we decided to fly home from our first port of call at St Thomas in the Virgin Isles. Andrew, our youngest was really poorly and despite the administration of a local doctor in St Lucia his condition was worrying. So we docked in St Thomas after a fairly unpleasant sea journey much relieved to be soon heading home.

Armed with passports, tickets and the newly introduced Access credit card I managed to eventually secure a taxi to the airport, leaving Margaret to pack and get the boys ready. Alas it was not to be, within several hundred yards from the airport we were halted by a mass demonstration of angry indigenous brightly dressed people all carrying banners and looking extremely distressed. Apparently, Trans World Airlines was rumoured to have gone into liquidation, thus the utter chaos and closure of the International Airport. As the ship was leaving that evening plans had to be abandoned, so I returned to the *Cunard Princess* and helped Margaret unpack.

The next port of call was Caracas in Venezuela, a long sea journey with two young children neither very well and a father suffering from seasickness. However, the seas had dropped to force eight and the hurricane forecast delayed so we settled to try and make the most of the journey.

Thus ensued my first and last experience of gambling. On the ship's top deck was a very salubrious casino. So, why not give it a try? After purchasing twenty five dollars of casino chips I immediately then lost ten dollars on the slots. Let's go for the big time! I had played pontoon at school and I gathered that blackjack was the same game under a different name. So I headed for the blackjack table complete with an elegant croupier, charming smile and with a body to convert a Trappist monk. There I sat, white dinner jacket, bow tie and a pile of chips - a real James Bond feel to the evening. All went well, in fact beyond belief, by eleven pm I had amassed a huge amount of bright white and blue casino chips in front of me, in fact enough to cover the whole holiday plus. A crowd was now massing round the table to watch the high roller beat the bank; my fifteen minutes of fame had arrived. "This is so easy", I said to myself and gestured to Margaret that I was on a roll and couldn't lose. What a feeling of power and success!! 'Pride before a fall.' Within seven minutes I had, through pure greed, lost the lot.

Next stop Caracas, so we duly arrived at La Guaira, the port of Caracas. The boys gaining mischievous ways as they settled into their new environment, however the Captain's warning of crime and danger on land made us decide not to take the family into danger as there had been several serious assaults on tourists. So forewarned I set off on my own to explore, find a local taxi and do a tour. What can go wrong? After several attempts I found a driver who spoke limited English. "U have a dollar", "Yes, I have US dollars". So off we go up the mountain, past extreme poverty and massive billboards advertising all sorts of commodities. Caracas itself is a mixture of extreme poverty and extreme wealth. However, the whole trip was quite sinister, being warned not to unlock the car doors and to try and avoid eye contact.

Without asking, Winston my Venezuelan driver informed me he was taking me to see his friend a local tradesman who sold amazing value gold jewellery. I was really getting anxious as we headed into the ghetto, which was really dark and threatening. We arrived in a dingy cul-de-sac and was ushered into a shanty-type workshop to meet Georges, the emaciated craftsman. To escape unscathed, I spent quite a large amount of US dollars to purchase a magnificent gold ring displaying a large gold nugget. With smiles and handshakes plus the somewhat unnerving warning not to declare the ring when rejoining the ship, we departed. Forty two years later the ring has never been valued, either a bargain or a fake?

The tour continued to a trip to the Ministry of Agriculture where I purchased a small crocodile, all above aboard and then a few more shops and back to the ship, safe and unscathed. Indeed quite an experience, well nearly …

I was arrested when declaring the crocodile. Apparently a well-known method of drug smuggling. Margaret slightly bemused when I phoned her about my delay. "Why did you buy a crocodile?" she asks with incredibility. "Because it helps the local economy." She hung up. While I waited at the dock for a decision to be made, I wondered what would happen if they found the gold. Luckily my crocodile got the all clear as the Ministry of Agriculture confirmed the paperwork given to me on purchasing it. I was allowed back on board, the crocodile still with us forty years later – stuffed of course!

We then travelled to Barbados, swam and lunched at Sandy Lane on the West Coast. Indeed one of the best days of our lives, where we have since returned many times. The rest of the cruise was uneventful apart from a small hiccup in Grenada. We had rented a villa for a day with a private pool at the newly-opened Spice Island Inn on Grand Anse beach and while we snoozed, the boys emptied the whole contents of a patio set, cushions included, into the plunge pool. We returned back home with a holiday never to be forgotten!

Majorca
Holiday from Hell

BACK IN THE EARLY seventies package holidays were in their infancy, so as an intrepid young family we booked an all-inclusive holiday in Majorca. The hotel Santa Lucia in Palma Nova seemed to offer all the facilities that we could want with two young children.

We had heard so much of the glories of the Mediterranean and indeed I had visited this quiet resort myself in the early sixties, so with fond memories looked forward to visiting again.

We arrived sadly to a jaded building, scruffy dirty rooms and public spaces that needed a complete makeover. The indoor swimming pool had beach chairs and broken glass on the bottom with the outdoor pool providing a display of two middle aged tattooed men urinating in it. Ushering the children quickly away, we headed to the dining room, alas little better as we were greeted by a glass cabinet with various plastic meals on display. One had to choose the appropriate numbered cards and take them back to your table. Then holding your chosen card overhead, the waitress brought the matching meal, usually cold, unappetising and inedible.

We had booked a family room but no such luck, however, as the children were not far away we settled for the night. Surely things must get better. Sadly not, we were awakened at 2 a.m. with loud hammering on the door and loud crashes against it. I rang Reception and frantically explained the problem; they just hung up on us. Fearing for the children, I tentatively opened the door to a fifty year old drunken Scotsman from Glasgow, sweating, smelling of alcohol and demanding for us to leave his room. After a short frightening conversation we worked out he was on the wrong floor. However, no sleep for us that night and no hotel security arrived.

The next day we took to the beach, mostly comprising of cigarette butts and dog excrement. We couldn't stay in this hell hole. However, the travel representative informed us we had to stay the week as there were no early flights home. We survived the week, eating out every night and spending as little time as possible in the horrendous hotel. On the final day we encountered a very sober Glaswegian who full of apologies gave the boys £10 each.

We have never returned to Majorca and indeed had fully forgotten of our ordeal until last summer when an elderly couple arrived in my studio on the Isles of Scilly and reminded us of our lucky escape. They had sat next to us on the plane over forty years ago, remembered our story and our invitation to visit us if ever on the Islands. Thus reminding us of our worst holiday ever!

The Grenadines – 1995
A Pleasant Breeze

HAVING BOOKED A HOLIDAY on a small Caribbean island in the Grenadines called Canouan, we were slightly disappointed to hear from our Travel Agent that the holiday was cancelled due to civil unrest. Apparently a Mr Donald Trump had recently purchased the island to create a golf resort, and unfortunately had employed foreign labourers from Italy. This was not acceptable to the local residents and indeed two Italians had been shot.

However, we were offered an alternative holiday on a very expensive private island at no extra charge. Young Island is situated a few hundred yards from St Vincent, the capital of the Grenadines, comprising of a limited number of exclusive dwellings with a fantastic private beach, with an amazing secluded natural rock swimming pool in the centre of the island surrounded by tropical palms and exotic plants.

We arrived at this island paradise by a small Islander plane, flying from Barbados to St. Vincent, then a short taxi ride to the small dock to be greeted by the ferryman to take us on the short trip to our destination. So exciting! Greeted with a rum punch on the dock by the Manager, we were taken to our luxurious apartment situated a few yards from the gently lapping Caribbean. Wow, thank you Mr Trump!

The first evening was magical, as we sat in a beachside Cabana with the sound of tree frogs; a fantastic meal was served notably with a choice of eight local breads that were straight from the wood oven to complement our shellfish delights. The highlight of the evening was yet to come. We were serenaded by one of the most delightful Tuk bands I have ever encountered, with three ageing West Indians playing an assortment of homemade instruments made out of broken bottles and biscuit tins. Wonderful sounds never to be forgotten. However, in midstream we were rudely interrupted, "move back immediately" these harshly spoken words ruining the peaceful ambience of the evening. "I'm sorry" I asked, "Why?" "You in de rifle sights man" (apparently two visitors had been shot that afternoon on St. Vincent, in retaliation for an American drug enforcement agency starting to destroy several cannabis farms on the mainland). We moved back very quickly and were slightly more circumspect about our change of venue.

Off to our lovely accommodation, we go to sleep listening to the gently lapping of the waves. A tropical storm hits the island at approximately 2 am. Very heavy torrential rain and heavy squalls, no problem, we soon went back to sleep after our tiring day. Waking up at 6 am, all did not seem quite right. I soon found out why, as I stepped out of the extremely comfortable bed into at least eight inches of water. Holy Moses we were sinking! Our suitcases were floating around the room. In fact, our villa was at the bottom of a steep embankment and the torrent had flooded our room.

A very apologetic management team soon arranged to dry our clothes and vacate us to the premier property on the island which was located at the very top, with panoramic views of all the Grenadines. Apparently, we were told that this normally cost five thousand dollars a night but to us no extra charge. It was truly a magnificent place and we soon settled in.

So now all settled, we set off to luxuriate on our private beach, silver sands with waiter service for drinks. All in all, the paradise that was advertised. Due to the exorbitant cost of the resort only a few other people frequented this oasis of calm. Sadly this only lasted for about half an hour! Our peace was dramatically shattered. From the air a squadron of US assault helicopters flew over at a very low altitude, fully manned with assault troops in full battle gear and ordnance. What in the hell was happening? Wave after wave flew over us; you would think we were in Vietnam, really terrifying. Surreally the waiters kept offering us refreshments, mostly in sign language because of the noise.

Approximately an hour later the noise slowly subsided, their mission now fairly obvious, as intense smoke emanating from St Vincent. They had destroyed the cannabis plantations that provided an illegal income for the indigenous islanders. Needless to say the DEA had not improved public relations for the innocent tourists. One slight bonus, the wind was in our direction!!! The rest of the day was completely uneventful, lunch, dinner and entertainment all magnificent so off to bed happy and settled.

Well until 3 am, when one is at one's deepest slumber, it's not the perfect solution to be awakened by the sound of voices and radio cackle emanating from under one's bed. Actually the house was built on stilts to deter termites which are extremely prolific in these latitudes. I very tentatively crept on to the balcony to be confronted by two armed security guards!!!! "Don't worry man, we only looking for de Semtex". Needless to say sleep was not forthcoming and the dawn was so welcoming. Only four more days to survive. As we had booked a package, the company would not let us escape any sooner. We still have a Christmas card from Young Island every year, but I don't think we will be returning!

Jet Lag
Look Before You Speak

WE HAD JUST COME to the end of a fairly traumatic sailing holiday on a forty foot bareback charter yacht called *Arianda*, sailing the British Virgin Islands in heavy winds and tumultuous seas! A mainsail stuck up the mast in the entrance to Road Town harbour with us drifting into the path of a very large cruise liner was not the least of our mishaps. We felt, at that point, that our bareboat sailing days were at an end!

During this time we were very fortunate to be on the staff travel concessions from our elder son, Andrew, that allowed us to take up unbooked seats on any schedule flight for a small charge. He suggested that there were several business class seats on flights back to London from New York. He would weight list us for them if we could get there. So as intrepid sailors and seasoned travellers we thought the chance was worth the risk for a comfortable flight home and duly set off on our journey!!

We caught the local ferry to the US Virgin Isles and then on with American Airlines to New York only arriving after a very turbulent flight, circling for forty-five minutes over New York due to a heavy snowstorm. Even the cabin staff had abandoned their duties, one actually came and sat next to us and vowed she'd not get up for anything!

Times Square, however, in summer clothing at midnight was not particularly pleasant but well worth it for that comfortable business class seat we were later to be snuggled into and the thought of champagne, delicious gourmet food and a good sleep on our way back home.

We love Times Square with its full on activity throughout both day and night and in no time at all we were kitted out in boots and warm clothing.

We set off to catch our flight home, checked in by great friendly staff, yes, seats still available ...

Fantastic, in fact euphoric, certainly well worth the trouble and extra expense.

We navigated our way through the airport and eventually got to the gate an hour early for our comfort and luxury ...

Alas, not to be ...

Fifteen emaciated supermodels had just checked in and as full fare paying passengers had been given our seats. We had been allocated the worse seats on the plane, next to the rest rooms and galley. The joys of staff travel!

No sleep, no champagne, no gourmet meal, no lying down. Back ache and general exhaustion instead! We were very relieved to arrive at Heathrow and stretch our legs.

Probably not in the best of humour, I stood to stretch my weary limbs only to be accosted by a very impatient fellow traveller wanting to get off the plane sooner!

He started tugging my shirt, then kept on tugging it. I ignored him until his consistency really annoyed.

Turning to him I told him, "Sit down, relax, you won't get get off any quicker. The doors are still shut, there's snow on the ground, early disembarkation is not going to happen."

I am told, since, that my voice got louder and louder, and was finally close to shouting, presumably as I had only just removed the earphones I had worn for the whole uncomfortable flight!

Needless to say, the cabin around me went very quiet (obviously in sympathy with me!!!) until the unfortunate passenger, a diminutive Indian gentleman, bravely spoke up. "I'm so sorry, Sir, but I think you are wearing one of my shoes." I look down and see that I, indeed, have one of his on and one of mine!

Deathly silence all around until Margaret starts uncontrollably laughing, followed by all the fellow passengers. I am left speechless!!!

No wonder the left shoe was so tight.

Next time I will swim home.

Dominica
The Escape

MARGARET AND I HAVE always been very happy with our own company. Although at home we have a very active social life which we really enjoy, on holiday we prefer our own privacy. We were slightly disconcerted when some friends turned up uninvited to our island retreat in Barbados. For many years we had stayed up in the hills in St Lucy overlooking the Caribbean. The Sugar Cane was the perfect retreat, so we were not really pleased to be swamped and organised by our so well intentioned friends.

A plan was quickly made and put into effect. (We would go on our travels and return when the coast was clear). A cunning plan evolved, so we bought a rover ticket on the local Caribbean airline, LIAT – not always trustworthy, but eventually they get you there.

Two days later we were landing on a small island airport, situated between mountains on a very difficult airline approach. Having arrived safely, we were transferred by a small bus on an extremely hazardous drive to the capital of Dominica, Roseau, a wonderful authentic Caribbean town, picturesque wooden balconied houses fronting the main street. It can only be described as the Jewel of the Caribbean. Indeed the whole island looked like a pristine garden centre.

We had booked into a beachside hotel called 'Castaways'. Dominica lacks beaches and we were on one of the few on the island, a patch of grey dirty sand, not particularly inspiring for sunbathing or swimming. However, we soon settled in, going to the beach barbeque and delighted to meet some friendly locals, one in particular after bumming some cigarettes from us, arranged for us to go whale watching the next day on the hotel's purported boat.

After a few drinks with us he offered to show us round Dominica. Crackerjack, as he was known had gone to school with the manager of the hotel, so we were surprised when the nephew of the owner sent him away, telling him to stay away from the hotel. Crackerjack as it turned out was a crack heroin addict with criminal tendencies – a lucky escape.

On the journey from Roseau to Castaways we had a lovely young taxi driver called Augustine; he was slightly worried about our intended hotel as he had heard some disturbing reports of staff unrest. The new American owner had dismissed all the local workers from the village and had replaced them with non-indigenous workers on a much lower pay scale. There could be trouble he informed us. He gave us his card and we promised to ring him if we encountered any problems.

Anyway, today was the whale watching adventure that we had come to the island to see. At the Roseau marina we had seen some fantastic boats, flying bridges, advanced speaker systems for the commentary and various forms of underwater cameras etc. They also had an open bar and of course a range of typically Caribbean snacks.

Our transport was picking us up from the hotel, thus saving us the expense of a taxi. We went down to the small seemingly derelict jetty, which was practically falling apart with several planks missing. No sign of our whale watching trip. Obviously, they would pick up the passengers from Roseau and then come for us.

A very old and decrepit fishing boat was moored to the jetty; we would have to climb over this when the tripper boat arrived. A heavily sunburnt emaciated Rasafarian with several missing teeth sat on the gunnels amid ships. "Room 17" he asked us. "Yes, we are waiting for our whale watching trip". "That's me, step aboard". What else could we do but join him on this foul, fish smelling apology for a boat. Indeed the whole scene could have come from a Hemmingway novel. "Just two more to come" he said, as he imbibed some noxious substance straight from an old rum bottle that had seen many a drink.

Two smartly dressed Americans arrived together with the Hotel Manager, this made us feel much safer. The Americans were obviously delighted to travel on such a mode of transport. "We so like to mix with the real residents," the brash husband told us ...

Off we went, the Calvin Ricardo engine firing on one cylinder only, emitting black smoke and making a loud bang every few minutes. We managed only about three hundred yards, the engine spluttered and then finally stopped. It sounded terminal. The sea was starting to get up, the boat had no safety equipment or life rafts.

Soldier, our boatman, oblivious to our concerns assured us that this was indeed the best spot to see whales. We watched the posh boats heading miles out to sea. What was going to happen next? Soldier really thought that we believed him and in fact he was going to give the engine a small service while we waited for the non-existent whales.

The open bar was provided, four bottles of Caribbean local beer, four bags of crisps that was the sumptuous buffet! By now the brash American was downing copious amounts of rum with the skipper. After two hours, we actually did see one whale tail and that was it!

Wait, a loud rushing and flapping sound was coming towards us, the sea looked as if it was boiling. Rastaman shouting with delight, heavens above, what a sight, surrounding us on all sides was a massive school of dolphins, hundreds of them, their large intelligent eyes staring at us. Quite a sight, never to be forgotten.

Soldier eventually got the antique engine started and we limped home bemused but happy after a different day in the sun.

Back on the jetty we found Augustine, he had heard and seen our experince from the shore and embarrased by his fellow countrymen, he arranged to pick us up at 6pm and show us some true Dominica hospitality. What a kind and thoughful young man. Pitch dark, 6pm arrived, Augustine as promised was waiting for us. Off we went, relaxed with anticipation for the evening ahead.

After twenty minutes driving we were begining to get slightly anxious, we were driving up into the rain forest and now there were no signs of habitation, even the dimly lit Chatel houses had begun to disappear. After another ten minutes, I was getting really apprehensive that we were being kidnapped, were we too trusting?

The doors had self-locked, but the windows were wide open so maybe we had some form of escape. The car was slowing, we had come to a dead end and emblazoned in the headlights was a mammoth rusting Coca-Cola sign about ten feet square.

The car stopped, we could go no further, was this really going to be a serious problem for us? Augustine smilingly opened the door for us and was joined by an equally smiling West Indian lady. Her name was Pearl, she was lovely, twenty-five stone of pure happiness.

She lived in a small chalet high in the rain forest with her young children. She had laid a table under a banyan tree, lit with coloured fairy lights and an immaculate white table-cloth, a meal of fresh crayfish straight from the river running next to her cabin. She informed us that this was the first time she had ever cooked for white people. A fantastic memory, a meal shared with Pearl and Augustine with a bottle of red wine provided by them, (real Dominican hospitality). We returned to Castaways a very relaxed and happy couple.

We awoke next morning to an austere total silence! Getting dressed we went looking for breakfast, no one to be seen. A completely empty hotel, abandoned, dishes not washed in the kitchen, cockroaches crawling over unwashed dishes.

We rang Augustine, 'Pack,' he said, 'under no circumstances go out, I will come and get you,' and his final words were, 'wear dark glasses,' The hotel had been placed under a voodoo curse. Everyone had fled including the Manager, who we later learned escaped by yacht to Antigua. Augustine came, we drove to Rouseau, and we fled to Antigua via private plane from a small cane field airstrip.

As we left the hotel two dubious West Indians were chatting, "You come to my island and I chop you!"

Voodoo in action! Folklore says if they can't see your eyes, they can't affect you.

Another day in paradise!

Antigua – 2007
Hoisted by my own petard

IN 2007 WE WERE very fortunate to be given staff travel concessions on a national airline by a family member which included accommodation at five-star hotels at very modest prices. So when visiting our younger son in the Virgin Isles we decided to treat ourselves to a premium hotel in Antigua for a luxury week.

The airline booking agent stressed that to get an outstanding suite we needed to be Returners. "Had we visited the hotel before?" In all honesty I answered "Yes", as I had visited the hotel to buy a pair of flip flops several years earlier. So she completed the form as a returning guest and as an aging gentleman she concluded that I must at least be an airline Captain! Before I could correct her error, the email was sent and the booking was made.

The journey started at Newquay airport where one of my wife's rich patients was forced to acknowledge us. Not really wanting to be seen with the xenophobic island craftsman, the brief encounter was ended as we boarded our plane for Gatwick. The next morning we arrived at Gatwick and checked-in early for our flight to Antigua. Alas Mr and Mrs Socially-Upward were also in the departure lounge, so sadly they had to acknowledge our presence and walk down the tunnel to the Boeing 747 entrance with us. With great relief we were informed by Mrs Socially-Upward that they would be leaving us, as they were flying Business Class. However, at this point the Cabin Service Director seeing our boarding cards and ignoring Mrs Socially-Upward, greeted us like long-lost friends, "seat 1a and 1b Mr & Mrs Bourdeaux." First class seats, approximately £3,000 per seat one way. Sadly Mr and Mrs Socially-Upward have never spoken since - how could the peasants afford such luxury? Indeed the £60 we had paid did seem very good value!

After a very pleasant flight we alighted at VC Bird Airport to be met by Winston, our toothless cannabis-smelling taxi driver, who despite his several antisocial habits had looked after us well on our previous visits and was always punctual. He had stopped trying to sell us various forms of contraband many years ago. Arriving at the hotel a smiling concierge carried our bags to Reception to check into our room. "Were we from Sergei Andropov's party?" A slight look of disappointment followed, as apparently the billionaire was expected with his private pilot who had just arrived in his private jet and a massive tip was normally forthcoming.

We checked in, and we were duly given a Returners upgrade. Captain and Mrs Bourdeaux waited to be escorted with their cases to their suite. I tried to explain that I didn't use the title of Captain, but the Receptionist was distracted by the arrival of the billionaire's private pilot in full uniform. Ignoring her, he took a quick glance at us old codgers and smilingly came across to shake our hands. All eyes were now on us. Who were these important people? Indeed, we ourselves were fairly perplexed, until the young pilot explained that he was a friend of our son, Andrew whom he had been chatting to while crossing the Atlantic, with Andrew flying the other way back from Bermuda. Having been given our descriptions he immediately recognised us.

Ensconced in our suite we chuckled at the mistaken impressions of our apparent wealth and fame that had been so incorrectly assumed over the past couple of days.

Anyway after a swim and a rum punch we could now relax and continue our break without further ado. Alas this was not to be, a knock on the door and a gold envelope was pushed under our door. An invitation to a 'Returners Dinner' was enclosed for Captain Bourdeaux and his wife. Being neither a genuine Returner nor an airline pilot, Margaret, my wife, decided enough was enough! She rang Reception immediately to say "that we couldn't attend," only to be told that "the dinner was in fact in our honour and the other invitations had been sent and accepted, so please change your minds", which we very reluctantly did.

There followed a select Champagne Reception for the twelve very pretentious selected guests with a memorable seven course dinner to follow – escargots, turbot with truffles, etc. Being seated between the Head of Sandals Resorts, who was there to discuss a purchase of the complete resort, and a fairly obsequious General Manager, I was able to hold them both in conversation without actually telling any falsehoods.

We survived this memorable evening with the one proviso, never ever again!

Tortola, West Indies – 2012
The Fugitives

TAKING THE LOCAL LIAT airline from Barbados was always a challenge. (Leave Island Any Time, as the locals say). Booking a hire car for collection at Terrance W Letts, Beef Island Airport, Tortola on a Sunday was not always possible. The local agent, Dell Obogo, whom I have known for some considerable time, has the Sunday off for a traditional family barbecue (usually comprising marinated goat served with rice and the strongest pepper sauce I have ever encountered). However, as a regular customer, he kindly left a Jimny jeep for me at the airport with the keys under the mat.

We arrived in heavy rain and once clearing the aggressive and very unfriendly immigration officials which seem to inhibit every country, we exited the terminal and soon found our jeep. As usual, Dell made a mistake with the keys but we eventually found them behind the sun visor. On a separate note, Margaret, my wonderful wife, has a first cousin in Cambridgeshire whose best friend was a specialist in traffic problems, dangerous driving, fraudulent paperwork, lack of insurance etc., who had been seconded to sort out the entire mobile infrastructure on the island. He relished the appointment, so heaven help any person that crossed his path with a traffic violation. Although, never having the displeasure of meeting him, I gather he was a total prat. At the time, I was on the Board of the Devon and Cornwall Police Authority, so was fully conversant with his brief. Anyway, that aside, we set off to Cane Garden Bay to stay with our younger son, Ben a commercial diver on the Island. He had lived there several years and was well known in the ex-pat community. A mix of really great people, although to be fair, with some dubious backgrounds. Indeed, at one notable dinner party I gather we sat with a bank robber, a hit man for the triads and a close confident of the Kray twins. I should add that these were charming people, well-educated and exemplary manners, with one having graduated from Marlborough College, and all from good family backgrounds.

After about a week of swimming and being entertained royally, I realised I had not settled the payment for the hire car. Just coming out of the sea and walking to the car to collect my clothes, my heart stopped. I had seen a sign on the car that did not quite ring true - Deedes 424-677xx. I immediately returned to Ben's house and rang Dell, "Car reg number H1317, is that your car?" "Not my car man" Dell retorted in a rather unexpected gruff voice, which was most unusual as he was a really laid back Rasta character. We had STOLEN a car and nonchalantly been driving around Tortola for a week, when the police had been the most active for several years. How delighted the seconded officer would be, to arrest a UK Police Authority member for stealing a car!!!!

We developed a cunning plan to return the said vehicle to the airport without being caught. Ben had instructions to ring anonymously the owner (we found his card in the glove box – would you believe he was called Deadman, a notorious local villain). Our mission was accomplished when we found the correct car with the help of a delightful police lady, in our naivety never thinking she might put two and two together and arrest us. Anyway, we returned safely to our embarrassed son, who having gently remonstrated with us, was ready to set off for work. Oh dear, we had left our keys in the stolen car! Ben drove to the airport at great speed and collected them before Deadman arrived to collect his car.

For the rest of the holiday we were treated like Bonnie and Clyde with a lot of street cred from Ben's friends and acquaintances. Quite a narrow escape and one embarrassed son. Karma perhaps?

British Virgin Islands – 2014
Christmas Afloat

WE HAD SPENT AN exciting week sailing in the British Virgin Isles, having chartered an aptly named thirty two foot Beneteau sailing boat called 'Passing Wind'. The exciting bit came when we took delivery of this monster, having never sailed anything bigger than my 16 ft. Wayfarer. To obtain the charter I had to exaggerate my abilities!!! No problem, I had been sailing since the age of ten, albeit in small racing dinghies. I didn't realise the change in scale could be so different and so many unforeseen challenges for the novice. Picking up fuel and water from a small jetty in force six winds just using the heads became a challenge, so many things to learn whilst all the time pretending all was under control.

Anyway we cast off in a very professional way without damaging anything, soon getting out into the main seaway and tentatively hoisting the sails. This really was the life! Now all we had to do was to make port on Marina Cay, a small island off Tortola. After several abortive attempts (all the places looked the same from the sea) we made port, moored up, got out the Merlot and after about an hour stopped shaking! Perhaps we should have hired a skipper?

Ben, our youngest turned up later for dinner in his fast inflatable and after a super evening departed arranging to meet us the next day at a place called Bitter End on the island of Virgin Gorda, opposite Richard Branson's Necker Island.

Another challenge for us intrepid sailors, but we made it! Sailing through the Colloquin reef, that on the local chart was marked caution, (many bareboat has been lost here) but today was Christmas, even though being in mid-February we were celebrating with Ben who had not had a family Christmas for several years. Margaret had brought a Christmas tree and a snowman, so there we were, miles off shore on a fairly safe anchorage. Drinks on shore at Sabre Rock to meet up with Ben who had been treasure diving for emeralds on the Anegada Reefs. An exciting meeting with a bronzed notorious Ben Gunn octogenarian called Bert Kilbride, a world famous treasure diver and millionaire on whom the film 'The Deep' was based on.

Well lubricated, we returned in high spirits to enjoy our feast. First step was to tie the dinghy to the bow so that we could light the barbecue. The previous night we had watched a brash American crew set fire to theirs. What a super party, a wonderful barbecue, lots of wine and Christmas music. Up to the bow to replace the dinghy and then off for a well-earned sleep. Oh dear, oh dear, no dinghy!!! Not what one wants! One mile off shore in a 32 ft. yacht pitch black and no means to get ashore, let alone several thousand dollars deposit lost.

Wait, I hear an outboard engine coming closer, I frantically wave my small torch to attract attention, it comes nearer so we can see the skipper. Ben hides, he knows the bloke and doesn't want to be embarrassed (such a help in a crisis).

No such problem for us, we were desperate, he came along side with his passengers and I explained our predicament. Cheekily in a laughing voice he asked us how many gin and tonics ago that was. Anyway, he promised to drop off his passengers and to come back to help, which he duly did. (Ben is still hiding).

Off we set in a ten foot dinghy and a small pencil torch to light our way in an inlet several miles wide. Luck was with us; about a mile away we encountered a brightly lit super yacht, probably 200 ft. long. Trailing astern six small dinghies with engines identical to ours. "There's my dinghy" I shout as we get closer. Not convinced, the young skipper sounded quite concerned as I leapt onto the ski platform at the stern of the yacht. He suggested I call the crew to say we were taking our dinghy. I tried but to no avail, it was three in the morning. "Are you sure," the young skipper asks.

"Definitely" I say, pointing out the John Bourdeaux pottery sticker on the bow, (just another way to embarrass Ben).

Just a slight hiccup, I promptly missed my footing and fell into the sea. (I'm sure it was nothing to do with the imbibed alcohol). Getting back on board, the engine started and thanking my rescuer, we set off back to our yacht. Obviously our predicament caught the ears of other moored yachts and as their navigation lights lit my path back, some wag started singing Christmas carols. By now, the inlet fully awake and Ben hiding in the scuppers.

A Christmas never to be forgotten!

Houston and Mexico – 2017
Sleepless in Texas

OUR YOUNGEST SON BEN has moved from the Virgin Isles and married a delightful young doctor in British Columbia, so this involves a change of venue for our Spring break. Rather than miss out on a warm and sunny break which we had become accustomed to in February, we decided to travel to Vancouver via Houston from where we would fly down to a picturesque fishing resort in Mexico called Cabot St Lucas. We had stopped off there several years ago and found a delightful hotel overlooking the marina. It had a roof top swimming pool and an exceptional restaurant. Ten days there would be the perfect break, before flying up to Vancouver from San Jose, Mexico.

Well planned, researched, costed, what could possibly go wrong?

The flight from Heathrow to Houston was totally uneventful, great business class seats, the flight time passing quickly and we were early. However, upon disembarking the plane, there was utter chaos, riots outside the airport, thousands (literally) queuing for immigration (despite a fully automated entry system) everybody being checked manually twice. None of the officials from Homeland Security seemed to have any clue as to what was going on - not helped by some not having a great grasp of the language, despite being in charge. We were trapped! Couldn't go forward or backward, we just had to be patient. What was happening?

Mr Donald Trump had today brought in the travel ban. Four hours later we were eventually cleared. I still feel that something on my passport caused extra security (Margaret is unsure of this). Being a proud Cornishman born in 'Camborne' and living in the Scilly Isles didn't help. Camborne on the Homeland computers shows up as Cambodia (do I look like a Pol Pot) then Scilly Isles could that be Sicily? (obvious Mafia connections).

Exhausted, however a really good night's sleep and ten days of sun would soon obliterate this trauma. Thanks to my mastery of the internet I had managed to book us into a hotel on the far side of Houston, adjacent to Hobby airport from where we would fly to Mexico.

The drive, which was approximately thirty minutes, gave us time to get to know the rather garrulous taxi driver who had settled in Houston some twenty years ago. He seemed rather mystified over our choice of hotel, but I explained, probably rather patronisingly, that we travelled a lot and always used this hotel chain.

On arrival at the hotel, he warned us "Not to leave the hotel under any circumstances, and ring for a cab if you want to go anywhere, even a few hundred yards". The reception area was not as bright and sparkling as many other of the hotel chain premises that I recalled (obviously due for refurbishment). A lot of rather seedy characters adorned the jaded lobby, in fact, probably a female sports team on a stopover and probably as tired as us, anyway very friendly, good eye contact so despite their scruffy apparel, no problem!

The Receptionist again looked not the part. No bra, fairly exposed accoutrements and a mini skirt so short that little was left to the imagination. However we were exhausted and she showed us to our ground floor apartment. Good heavens, it was disgusting!! Unmade bed with an unpleasant odour emanating from the sheets, a large picture window (filthy) looking onto a concrete wall decorated with fairly obscene graffiti. What had we come to? Staff quarters perhaps? Obviously the wrong room.

Tired, I left Margaret with the cases and tentatively went to talk to the bra-less wonder about a change of room. I explained it was a special occasion and I wanted a really nice room for the lovely lady I was with. No problem, "We have a special suite which I am sure will meet your needs". So off I go to the elevator with Rosita as she insisted on me calling her. A minuscule elevator, a half-naked woman, smelling of the strongest scent I had ever smelt, was not what my Sunday school teacher had prepared me for (especially at midnight in a foreign country).

Without further ado we arrived at the Penthouse, brushing past me she swung open the door, "Our best suite" she boasts. Alas, with the exception of a bubbling Jacuzzi in the corner, it was just as squalid as the former. We couldn't stay here!! Apologetically, I extracted my wallet. I am sure she would call a cab, no refund needed; we just needed to get out. Oh dear!! She sadly misinterpreted my generous gesture. "No problem honey, you'd like some extra company, Jacinda should suit you well". The haze lifted, it all became clear, and we had booked into a house of ill repute!! A Texan brothel no less.

Trying to explain the misunderstanding was not a problem. I collected my lovely Margaret and us two intrepid pensioners stood outside a Texan whorehouse in the rain at 1am waiting for a taxi driver who spoke English (many only spoke Mexican in Houston). We were later admitted to a Holiday Inn as 'walk ins'. What a relief!

Another day tomorrow.

Cabo San Lucas, Mexico – 2017
Exciting Times

HAVING HAD A TRAUMATIC experience in a pre-booked hotel in Houston, we escaped at 1am to eventually find sanctuary in a Holiday Inn apartment. After managing three hours sleep, we then took a taxi to Houston Hobby airport to check-in.

Being in plenty of time to catch our flight to San Jose in Mexico, all now should be well and our vacation in the sunny fishing resort on Cabo San Lucas in Mexico could hopefully begin. Several years ago we had discovered the delightful fishing village and marina of Cabo San Lucas. Back then, we had found a lovely hotel in the centre of the marina, with a rooftop pool and a fantastic alfresco restaurant. Our first trip there was fairly short (six hours) but we were returning to really relax and enjoy our previous discovery.

On entering the airport we were faced with a bank of sinister electronic machines designed to print our luggage labels and boarding passes. So with great trepidation we braced ourselves for the forthcoming challenge. Alas, after several attempts and total frustration we decided to ask for help. Not so easy, the preoccupied staff were still in shock after the chaos caused by the implementation of the Trump travel ban the day before. It seemed the last thing anyone wanted to do, was to help two foreign pensioners. I should add most of the staff seemed to be of Mexican origin with limited English and we spoke no Spanish.

However, all was not lost as a friendly American lady took us in hand and guided us to a serviced check-in desk explaining that all the machines were malfunctioning. They were so helpful and after a few hiccups we trailed off to join the queue for the security check to get to our gate on time.

Due to the enhanced security we stood and shuffled for at least half an hour. At last, at the pit face we nonchalantly presented our boarding cards and passports to the rather surly official. He immediately took on an excited smile and started pointing and waving us away from the gate. His colleagues explained to us in good humour – the Gringos passes were not in order, go back and check in again. Apparently, the boarding pass inferred that we were in San Francisco not Houston. A total impossibility! We were here standing next to him in Houston, but Mr Jobsworth refused to let us through. So off back to the check-in desk to try and correct the error (perhaps we had become time travellers?)

Sorted at last with the right boarding pass, we returned to the queue which was now probably a hundred yards long (we would not make our flight). Since a child I had learned to avoid many problems, be it Latin tests, or cross country runs on a cold day, by inventing small illnesses that precluded and circumvented the problems. Now guile was needed, finding our lovely lady again and explaining that I had recently had open heart surgery (true) could she help us get to the gate in time for our flight. No problem, escorted through the VIP channel and bypassing the smiling Jobsworth, we made the gate and boarded the plane. Settled into a comfortable seat and cruising at 35,000 feet the traumas of the last twenty-four hours seemed a lifetime away.

Arriving in San Jose we were warned before leaving the plane not to use any forms of technology inside the terminal building.

If we did, phones etc., would be confiscated and not returned, indeed we could be arrested, (to this day we have never understood this ruling) What a strange welcome. We then had to run the gauntlet of several tens of Mexicans trying to sell us trips timeshares, restaurant reservations, tours and taxis. Welcome to Mexico, where the average wage is approximately ten dollars a day for these impoverished people who had to live on their wits (No wonder the mass exodus to USA?) That being said, we then had to haggle for a taxi with prices ranging from twenty dollars to one hundred. We settled for thirty and had a pleasant drive to the marina and our hotel. Just as we remembered it, actually not quite! After checking in and being escorted to our fabulous apartment overlooking the marina, we quickly changed and made our way to the rooftop pool and amenities of which we had such fond memories.

On our previous visit this was a calm and tranquil place of luxury, alas no more. Loud pop music, every deck chair taken with what seemed a Mexican Mafia Convention. The Sopranos and Corlioni family all greased and splayed in the Mexican sun. Very large cigar smoking gentlemen, ladies very thin with six packs and enormous false breasts. The immaculately dressed pool attendant and Maitre D' found us a chair and explained that this was a public holiday and things would soon return to normal. The final end to our arrival day was seeing two very attractive young ladies making out in the Jacuzzi. We escaped and found a lovely restaurant a few hundred yards from the hotel had a great meal, imbibed some lovely wine and went to bed.

The next morning we awoke bright and early and decided to explore Cabo. After an amazing rooftop breakfast we set off. Everyone in the marina and town were exceptionally friendly. One young man hailing us as long lost friends, how are you settling in to the Tessorro, our hotel? He told us he worked there and indeed checked us in. This gave us a feeling of safety and he went on to tell us of his several jobs. Indeed with his help – whale watching, snorkeling, trips to various places could be obtained at well under half price. His brother owned a boat; meanwhile could we please help him.

He had a proposition for us; we could have a free trip with breakfast at a fantastic new resort up the coast. On top of this, he would share his introductory commission with us, as long as we had two major credit cards, a passport and already owned a timeshare. We had agreed to listen to a one hour presentation, no obligation as we said no way would we be purchasers. No problem, just help me and I will give you two hundred US dollars on completion. As he was linked to the hotel, we felt completely safe and as we had nothing else planned, why not?

Eight am the next morning, Angelo picked us up and off we went to The Grand Mayan, a brand new complex. Angelo handed us over to a slick American who took us to breakfast and then proceeded with the hard sell. After ninety minutes a disgruntled American gave up and sent us on our way (he was not happy). However, he had not finished with us. Suffice to say he directed us to collect our cash reward but we ended up in an underground cellar and we could find no way out until a waiter who had just been sacked showed us the way out.

With his help we found Reception and collected two hundred dollars and got a taxi home. Through various other contacts of Angelo we continued this morning charade for several more days accumulating several hundred US dollars. We had made fantastic profit and all our trips had been paid for by our exploits.

Just one more escapade and retire. I should say that Angelo assured us that it was all completely above board as seventy five per cent of Americans made a purchase. (We have since heard that Cabo was considered the timeshares capital of the world, providing millions of pounds of revenue for the drug lords, who had started investing millions in the property market. a sure and safe way of laundering money). I should say we only learnt this in retrospect.

The day arrived, this time things seemed slightly more sinister. We were passed via three different groups arriving at a derelict building on the outskirts of the marina fish market. We were taken down a series of alleys to a dimly lit café for the pre sales breakfast. However, this morning's host was slightly more intense. Patiently explaining to us that this was a different type of investment, indeed he called it a concept. Slightly perplexed we followed him again through the backstreets until we found ourselves next to a derelict building, up the fire escape into a small bare office where a jaded young lady checked our credentials. "When will we be visiting the property" we asked Ignoring our question she ushered us into a room approximately fifty square feet completely bare with the exception of a table. four chairs and a computer. A very tough looking woman rose to meet us. Her handshake was like a mole grip "Right let's get to business" she said and started to fire off a series of personal questions about our personal finances and lifestyle. After about an hour she started to flag as we reciprocated by asking her some searching questions. She was actually trying to sell a lifestyle concept, not even a property! She then called in her breakfast hitman who tried for another hour, how could we escape? Now two hours had passed and we weren't quite sure where we were.

"Well" I said not wanting to offend and indeed the whole atmosphere had got quite sinister our hosts' body language was now not being particularly friendly "I am interested" I said "I am not saying a definite no or yes". This left them in a slight quandary. Being such simple and gullible old English people, they had not given up. They let us go with four hundred dollars in our wallet, (our best so far) We left them hoping that we would contact them the next day

Returning to the Tessorro I chatted to one of the Mafioso who liked our English accents. I explained our week's adventure slightly needing approbation. He then proceeded to frighten us. Angelo did not know us. We were wearing the hotel tags on our wrists so everyone knew where we were staying. Angelo was probably part of a well organised gang of Mafia con merchants. Tomorrow we would receive a tremendous final offer, as to date all promises had been fulfilled. Thus we had total confidence. "Tell me" he said, "I bet you, at present you have in your possession your credit cards, passports and at least a thousand dollars in cash. Is that correct?" Sheepishly, I confirmed his suspicions.

"Tomorrow' he said 'you will be picked up for your usual breakfast. However, they will drive you into the desert, steal all your money, passports etc. They will leave you there until eventually you are rescued. I assure you no facial recognition will be possible as we all look the same." With a pat on the back and a smile. "Have a nice day".

Had this fellow resident saved our lives? Was he involved? We did not leave the hotel for two days, cut off all communications and we were very relieved to fly to Vancouver two days later.